BREATHING CORPSES

Laura Wade
BREATHING CORPSES

OBERON BOOKS
LONDON

First published in 2005 by Oberon Books Ltd
521 Caledonian Road, London N7 9RH
Tel: 020 7607 3637 / Fax: 020 7607 3629
e-mail: info@oberonbooks.com
www.oberonbooks.com

Reprinted in 2006, 2010, 2011 (twice)

A catalogue record for this book is available from the British
Library.

ISBN: 978-1-84002-546-0

Cover image by Ben Curzon/Research Studios

Printed and bound by CPI Group (UK) Ltd, Croydon, CR0 4YY

When a man has lost all happiness, he's not alive.
Call him a breathing corpse.

SOPHOCLES

ACKNOWLEDGEMENTS

My heartfelt gratitude to these people, who were crucial to the development of *Breathing Corpses*: Charlotte Mann and Rod Hall; Tamara Harvey; Jack Thorne; Michael Shaw; Tina and Stuart Wade; Nina Steiger; Sacha Wares; Nina Lyndon, Emily McLaughlin, Simon Stephens and the Royal Court YWP; Nikolas Kamtsis and all at Interplay Europe 2004; Neil McPherson; Jack Andrews and the Pearson Playwrights panel; plus Anna Mackmin, Ian Rickson, Graham Whybrow and all at the Royal Court.

Thank you.

LW, February 2005

Characters

AMY
19, a hotel chambermaid

JIM
45, manager of a self-storage facility

ELAINE
46, Jim's wife

RAY
26, an employee at Jim's self-storage site

KATE
35, runs her own business

BEN
28, Kate's live-in boyfriend

CHARLIE
30, a hotel guest

Breathing Corpses was first performed on 24 February 2005 at the Royal Court Jerwood Theatre Upstairs with the following company:

AMY, Laura Elphinstone
JIM, Paul Copley
ELAINE, Niamh Cusack
RAY, Ryan Pope
KATE, Tamzin Outhwaite
BEN, James McAvoy
CHARLIE, Rupert Evans

Director, Anna Mackmin
Designer, Paul Wills
Lighting Designer, Mark Jonathan
Sound Designer, Ian Dickinson

SCENE 1

Tuesday morning, late January, cold but bright.

A hotel room. Not a great hotel, a mid-price hotel that trades on its views over the town rather than its quality of service.

Someone is lying in the bed, the sheets pulled up high. The figure is absolutely motionless.

AMY comes into the room with clean towels over her arm and a plastic carry-case of cleaning fluids. She is wearing a black skirt and white shirt, with a burgundy tabard over the top. She has rubber gloves on her hands.

She stops short when she sees there is someone in the bed.

AMY: Oh god, sorry.

> *She goes to back out of the room, then stops again. She turns back slowly for a longer look at the figure in the bed.*

Right.

God not again.

> *She looks away. Bites her lip.*

You're supposed to put the Do Not Disturb on. Then I wouldn't come barging in.

> *AMY takes a breath and goes over to the bed. She lifts the sheet and looks under it.*

OK.

> *She replaces the sheet. She sees a pill bottle on the bedside table and picks it up. It's empty.*

OK.

> *Beat.*

> *AMY lifts the sheet and puts one of her hands to the forehead of the body underneath. She frowns, unable to feel the temperature through her gloves.*

She takes off one glove and touches the forehead with her hand.

Yeah.

She lifts the figure's arm out from under the sheet and puts her fingers to its wrist. She looks at her watch with her other hand. A moment.

Yeah.

She lets the arm drop and it falls, lifeless. She watches, interested, then picks it up again and drops it. And again.

Yep.

AMY carefully puts the arm back under the sheet. She puts her rubber glove back on.

She goes over to the dressing table and sits on the stool, looking at the bed. She puts a hand to her mouth and looks around the room.

She goes to the phone by the side of the bed and picks it up, never taking her eyes off the body. She starts to dial, then changes her mind and puts the receiver down.

She sits back down on the stool and makes a sound like crying. She stops herself almost instantly.

Shit. Sorry. Sorry.

She looks to the bed momentarily, as if the corpse said something.

I'm OK.

AMY wipes her eyes and smiles weakly.

Just– you're dead and I'm going to get sacked I think, so– Not very– not very good, is it?

She laughs at herself.

Talking to you.

She frowns, looking around the room.

That's new.

She sighs and turns back to the corpse.

What's your name, Mr Man?

She turns back to the bed, pretending that the corpse spoke.

I'll go down and tell them in a minute. Probably think I'm joking this time.

Beat.

AMY sees an envelope propped up on the dressing table.

Oh, you did a letter. Nice.

AMY picks the envelope up.

You know you look– I bet you were lovely. I bet you were really– really kind.

Not a person I'd ever really talk to but. But you look lovely. Don't fancy you or anything, you're a bit old for me. Probably got kids my age. Oh god have you got–

Beat. She looks at the envelope.

Does it say in here? Who's Elaine?

She turns the envelope over in her hand.

You didn't lick it. You know they'll take this. Evidence. She'll not get it for days. She'll have a few days of not knowing why, while they're doing tests on it and stuff. If you've said why in here.

D'you mind if I– It's just you've not sealed it, so no-one'd know, cept you and me and I won't tell anyone if you don't.

AMY opens the letter and turns it over to see the name at the bottom.

Jim. Hi Jim.

She reads the letter.

Oh my god. A woman in a *box*. Like a cardboard box? God. Yeah, that's really hard. Hard enough finding you, can't imagine if I found one in a box.

Didn't you wonder about who was going to find you?

AMY finishes the letter.

That's a really nice letter, Jim. I mean, you know… For that kind of letter it's nice. Not too long, you don't blame anyone. Wouldn't seem fair, really, they never get chance to say anything back. Good you haven't blamed anyone.

D'you mind if I open the window? It's just you smell a bit. No offence, but. It's just– You've had a stressful time, what with the– (*Gestures to the letter.*) and I think you've– on the sheets, so–

She opens the window.

Cold out there.

Don't want to smell nasty when they come in, do you? Least it's winter, you'd smell worse if it was summer. Did you mean to wait till after Christmas, did you think about that?

AMY looks out of the window.

See the park from here. Best view, this one.

Will you miss the sky, d'you think?

She turns back to the bed, her hand to her mouth.

Beat.

She goes slowly back to the bed and lifts the sheet to look at the body's face.

Oh, you've been– You're all red, round your eyes.

She puts the sheet back, and then thinks for a moment before sitting on the side of the bed.

Well I can't clean up now, can I? Least you didn't sick up on yourself, quite tidy really.

She reaches for the corpse's hand and holds it in her lap.

There you go.

Cold hands.

She looks intently at the back of the corpse's hand.

How old d'you have to be before you get the brown spots?

Pause. She goes to the end of the bed, lifts the sheet from the corpse's feet and looks at them. She touches the top of one of them lightly, then looks at the door. She sits back, thinking.

You know what gets me? Why wouldn't you go somewhere really good? Cause you're not going to have to pay for it next morning, are you? Why wouldn't you book into somewhere really posh, the Ritz or the Hilton or something, that's what I'd do. Get a bus to London, new credit card cause you'll not be around to pay the bill, will you? See a show. Have a nice long jacuzzi and then fall asleep forever but– But least it's a nice four-poster, Egyptian cotton. Chocolate on the pillow. Not a hotel on a bloody roundabout in this bloody shithole, nice plants in the lobby but if there's chocolate on the pillow means I didn't clean your room before you checked in. And it might not be chocolate...

AMY looks over at the tea-tray on the dressing table. She goes to it and picks up the tea cup.

Had a cup of tea, at least.

I'd like to do that. Something mad. Not. Not top myself but– Go somewhere. Far away in a fast car.

She looks back at the tray.

Didn't touch the shortbreads, I'm not surprised.

AMY looks out of the window.

Why would you not– Why wouldn't you think there was something *better* coming for you?

Like a person to come and drive you away, out of your life or.

Or something. You could wait for.

Most days all I want at the end of it's a sit down. A walk in the park even. Someone who wet shaves and likes buying me stuff and isn't a bastard like my dad. Someone to talk to.

She looks over at the corpse.

That's not dead.

Just cause you found a body you lost all your *hope*? That's it? What the bloody hell's going to happen to me, then?

AMY sighs. She moves back to the bed and sits on the end. She takes the corpse's foot in both her hands and looks at it. She rubs her hands over the foot slowly and then massages it, tentatively at first then with more confidence.

After a few moments she puts the foot down.

I think I will get the boot this time.

She picks up the other foot and massages it as she speaks.

You weren't to know.

They don't think I did it, not real– although I did get questioned last time cause they found my fingerprints on the bottle next to the bed, got in trouble for what was it, disturbing a crime scene– Manager says I'm the angel of death. Don't know why it's always me.

I mean, I do– I do think there's something wrong with me, there must–

She looks away, close to tears, then smiles.

Why can't the thing that makes me different be a nice

thing? Special cause I'm I don't know pretty or something. Someone people'd want to look after.

Stupid cow.

Beat.

I should go then. Go tell them. Not good to leave it too long.

She looks at the bed.

I hope you have a nice time. I don't believe in God, really, which is a shame in this type of situation, but–

AMY leaves the room, feigning hurry.

Fade.

SCENE 2

Monday afternoon, mid-December, heavy rain.

The reception area at Green Door Self-Storage. It's very brightly/ artificially lit, bright colours, lots of green. A service counter with a computer behind it. A rack of padlocks and packaging materials (parcel tape, rolls of bubble wrap, flat-packed boxes) stands to the side.

JIM stands behind the counter, surveying the area. He's wearing a checked shirt and khaki trousers – the boss, but not a suit. He goes round to the front of the counter and looks at a printed notice sellotaped to it: 'This weeks offer: sign up for 7 weeks storage, get the 8th for FREE'.

He frowns, takes the poster down and adds apostrophes with a black marker, then sticks it back up: 'This week's offer: sign up for 7 weeks' storage, get the 8th for FREE'.

He goes to sit behind the counter and straightens the boxes of leaflets standing on it. He takes out a glossy catalogue and reads.

The door opens from the car park and JIM puts his catalogue behind the counter, out of sight.

ELAINE and RAY enter, dripping with rain. ELAINE is mid-story, RAY is listening. She is smartly dressed under her raincoat, has made an effort. RAY wears the Green Door Self-Storage uniform – green dungarees and baseball cap.

ELAINE: …so I'm trying not to panic, but I'm starting to panic, and I'm thinking well I'd better ring Sky. But the way you ring them is you bring the number up on the screen and I can't get any of these buttons to work so I'm stuffed basically… Hi Jim.

JIM: Everything alright?

ELAINE: Ye-es. Yes.

JIM: You sure?

ELAINE: Thought I'd pop in and say hello. (*Taking her raincoat off.*) Miserable out there, found this one out in it, pushing trolleys around, silly boy.

JIM: I asked him / to–

ELAINE sits on a high stool in front of the counter, her legs crossed.

ELAINE: I said you'd want him to stop now it's siling down.

JIM: You just popped in to–

ELAINE: I missed you, gorgeous.

ELAINE mimes a kiss towards JIM, then turns back to RAY who leans awkwardly on the end of the counter, listening to her. JIM goes back to reading.

(*To RAY.*) …anyway, I have to ransack the house and I finally find the number to call and before she's even even asked my account number or code or anything I'm going 'I can't get my TV to work, it's just not working, I can't get it to work'. So the girl on the other end she's got this everso calm voice and she's saying 'Alright, calm down, OK, calm down' and I calm down and she's going 'Now what can you see?' and I tell her and she asks me if the light's on on the remote and I say 'Yes, yes but it's red and I can't get it to go green' so she goes 'OK, this is what I want you to do – go to the Skybox–' You got one of these, Ray?

RAY: Er. Yeah.

ELAINE: Cause it's all a bit of a mystery to me this little box, only the kids know how to work it so now they're off at college– anyway, she says she wants me to find the, the power cable, which I do and she says 'OK, I want you to unplug it'. And I'm / thinking–

JIM: Hang on to your socks, Ray, punchline's coming.

ELAINE: Shut up. I'm. Jim. (*Back to RAY.*) I'm thinking that sounds a bit drastic so I say 'God, are you sure' and she's really firm saying 'Yes – unplug it'. So I unplug it and she tells me we have to leave it alone. For a minute.

So we sit there on the phone in silence for a whole minute – feels like forever, you know how a minute's silence feels–

17

JIM: Never get one with you…

ELAINE: You know what I– Jim. You know what I mean, Ray?

RAY: Um, yeah.

ELAINE: Cause you can just hear the other person breathing, if I was her I'd be typing or something just to make some noise, but she doesn't she just sits there and I'm sitting on the floor this end with the plug in my hand and I've never been more *aware* of myself. I'm getting more and more panicky and she says she says 'You still there' and I say 'yes' and then we're back to feeling out the length of this minute and then finally – finally finally finally – we get to 60 seconds and she says 'OK, here's what I want you to do. I want you to–

ELAINE pauses momentarily for effect. JIM doesn't look up from his reading.

JIM: Plug it back in again.

ELAINE: Plug it back in again!

RAY laughs. Briefly.

Thanks.

JIM: No, thank you. Suddenly my day seems all productive and worthwhile.

ELAINE: Well the point *is*, the point is it made me think I should probably get out a bit. Pop in and see you at work sometimes…

JIM: God help us. Don't stand there, Ray, she'll start another.

RAY: Right. Um, can I–

ELAINE: Anyway it's broken again now so–

JIM: Fill that rack, yeah…

RAY: Yeah.

JIM: …while I put my wife back in her box.

ELAINE: What you doing's so important, then?

JIM: Reading.

ELAINE: Yeah, what?

> *ELAINE leans over the counter trying to see what JIM is doing. He moves it so that she can't see.*

JIM: Work, alright?

RAY: What d'you think, though?

> *ELAINE leans over to try to have another look.*

JIM: Oy. (*To RAY.*) Bout what?

RAY: Y'know...

JIM: Oh. Yep, funny smell.

ELAINE: What's this?

RAY: Really funny.

JIM: Not *really* funny, no.

RAY: Don't you think?

JIM: Not really, no.

RAY: You don't think we should have a look?

JIM: Need more reason than a funny smell to go busting stuff open, dipstick.

ELAINE: Bust what open?

JIM: Bit of a funny smell coming off one of the units / that's all.

RAY: Very funny smell.

JIM: Ray.

RAY: Like–

ELAINE: Like what?

RAY: Nothing. Funny.

JIM: I'll give the guy a call.

RAY: You see the size of the padlock?

JIM: No accounting for people, paranoia... I'll give him a call.

JIM looks at RAY.

RAY: Right. Yeah.

RAY goes out.

JIM: Put him in charge of security accessories. Think I'd given him a badge and a gun, the way he's– Did you have to go on about Sky?

ELAINE: He laughed.

JIM: Not the point.

ELAINE: You shouldn't call him dipstick, he's got no confidence already–

JIM: Do yourself down, sounds like you sit at home all day with your feet up.

ELAINE: I pretty much do, love, now the boys are gone...

JIM: Got to call this bloke.

ELAINE: Came in cause I missed you.

JIM: Right.

ELAINE: Sorry.

Beat. RAY comes back in, a box of padlocks in his hand. Sees there's an atmosphere.

RAY: Sorry, I–

JIM: No, no. You get on.

RAY: Right. Boss–

ELAINE: D'you ask him to call you boss?

JIM: Just a joke, office joke.

ELAINE: You can call him Jim, you know.

JIM: He knows.

ELAINE: I call him fathead sometimes, but it's affectionate, isn't it?

RAY: Right.

RAY goes over to the display rack and puts the box of padlocks down by it. He looks at the box, lost in thought.

ELAINE rummages in her bag.

ELAINE: Here – I brought you something. Stopped off to get you a bacon sarnie. Extra red sauce.

She hands JIM a sandwich in a paper bag, then rummages again and pulls out another.

JIM: It's three in the afternoon.

ELAINE: I know, but– I don't know. Shouldn't watch the news, really. Made me want to come see you, bring you something. Don't have to eat it.

JIM: You watched the news?

ELAINE: I do sometimes. Not much else on cause of them capturing um– Bacon sarnie, Ray?

RAY: Oh. Cheers.

ELAINE hands RAY the second paper bag.

JIM: Capturing who?

ELAINE: Hussein.

JIM: Saddam?

ELAINE: Yep.

JIM: Hussein's his first name, they do it the other way / round.

ELAINE: Found him hiding in a hole. I didn't get you any red sauce, Ray, didn't know if you liked it.

RAY: Ah thanks.

JIM: Where?

RAY: I do like it. Red sauce.

ELAINE: Remember next time.

RAY: Got some in the kitchen…

JIM: A hole where?

RAY goes out.

ELAINE: Desert somewhere. Little hole in the ground, like a little mole or something.

You going to call that man, then?

JIM: You've just given me a bacon sarnie, I'm not doing anything.

JIM eats his sandwich.

ELAINE: Imagine being the soldier walking up to that hole and not knowing two minutes later you'd have saved the western world. Imagine that.

JIM: Uh-huh.

ELAINE: Like when the doorbell's rung – that bit where you're walking to the door and you don't know who it is yet.

Ketchup on your face, love.

Funny, though. Doesn't look like he'd kill millions of people.

JIM: (*Eating.*) Wha?

ELAINE: Remember thinking that last time, always think he's got a really kind face.

JIM: He's a dictator.

ELAINE: Doesn't look it, though, does he?

JIM: I think they've a fair bit of evidence, it's not difficult.

ELAINE: I know, but. Like the time before, when he was on telly with all the little kids.

JIM: Hostages.

ELAINE: Seemed really nice, patting them all on the head. Like an uncle.

RAY comes back in. Takes a knife from his pocket and starts to open the box of padlocks with one hand, his sandwich (now oozing ketchup) in the other.

RAY: Did you call him, boss? That bloke.

JIM: Not yet. After I've eaten this.

RAY looks at ELAINE. ELAINE looks at JIM.

Chuffing hell. Do it now, then.

JIM goes into the office behind the counter.

ELAINE: Alright Ray?

RAY: Yeah. Mrs–

ELAINE: Elaine. Mrs Boss if you like. Chief of padlocks, eh?

RAY: Yeah.

ELAINE: Well done.

RAY: Thanks, I– Thanks.

ELAINE: You'll do well, be good at that.

ELAINE leans over the counter.

What's this he's reading then?

She picks up a catalogue and looks at it.

23

Golden Moments. Give the gift of an exciting day out. Bloody hell. Have you seen this, Ray?

RAY: Yeah. I like the–

ELAINE: God the things you can do – ballooning, bungee jumping, fly a fighter plane, god listen to this – Fly a MIG fighter plane…

RAY: Yeah.

ELAINE: …Fly to Moscow day 1 and spend the day relaxing and sightseeing. Day 2 you are fully briefed and trained for your thirty minute flying experience. Thirty minutes! Seems a long way to go for half an hour of fun, doesn't it?

RAY: Yeah.

She flicks through further.

ELAINE: Oh, there we are, Day at a Health Spa, that's it. Ray, if he's getting one of these for me it's the health spa, not the fighter jet, alright?

RAY: Bungee jump, maybe.

ELAINE: Rather stick pins in my eyes. You could, though, young enough…

RAY: Nah. Don't really–

ELAINE is looking over the counter again.

ELAINE: Ooh, there's chocolates here.

She pulls out a box of Celebrations, two thirds full. Closes her eyes and puts her hand in. Pulls out a chocolate and looks at it.

Pff. Malteser.

She eats it anyway.

Chocolate, Ray?

RAY is about to take one when JIM comes back in. ELAINE holds the box out of sight.

RAY: Yeah?

JIM: No answer. Try later.

> *RAY goes back to the padlock rack. ELAINE and JIM stare out at the car park.*

ELAINE: Still raining, then.

> *ELAINE leans over the counter to put the chocolate box back.*

Bit quiet, isn't it?

JIM: Afternoon. Low period.

ELAINE: So bloody quiet in the house. Empty nest.

JIM: Danny's back tomorrow.

ELAINE: He's not actually.

JIM: Oh.

ELAINE: Couple of parties and things he wants to go to next week, so– Well it's more exciting there than being with us old sods, isn't it? Understandable he'd want to stay, probably all stay a bit after the end of term, promised he'd be back well before Christmas day.

JIM: When?

ELAINE: Twenty-third. Same as Mark. Get them both a few days at least.

> *They look out at the car park.*

Understandable, isn't it?

> *Beat.*

Doesn't seem fair.

JIM: No.

> *RAY is intent on the padlock rack. JIM looks over and sees that he's not looking, then leans over the counter and kisses ELAINE on the cheek.*

ELAINE smiles, still looking out.

RAY is staring at a padlock in his hand. He makes a decision and turns to JIM.

RAY: What was his name?

JIM: What?

RAY: B Sixteen.

JIM looks at the computer.

JIM: Ben Elliott. You did the form, it says here.

RAY: Ben Elliott. What's he look like?

JIM: I dunno Ray, you served him, we don't put a description on.

RAY: Did he have a dog?

ELAINE: You think he's put a dog in there?

RAY: No, just– Nothing.

JIM: Ray?

RAY: (*To ELAINE.*) Can't stash something alive, says in the storage agreement. Nothing that'll decompose. (*To JIM.*) Remember the kebab van?

JIM: Yeah.

ELAINE: A kebab van?

RAY: Go on, you tell it better than me.

JIM: Man has kebab van, I've told you this story–

ELAINE: No, tell me.

JIM: Well he buys a job lot of those elephant leg things–

RAY: Doner kebab.

JIM: – and he can't fit them in his van so he hires a unit, doesn't tell us what he's putting in and it's a plain enough box, it's not like it's from a legitimate supplier. Then his van gets stolen and he forgets all about these bloody kebabs, goes back to live with his mum in Wigan. First we know about it, four weeks later, the smell gets you every time you go–

RAY: Cause that unit's just there, just behind the office–

JIM: Am I telling this or–

RAY: Sorry.

JIM: So I think it's a dead bird on the roof for a while, didn't do anything about it. Don't realise it's A Five till the maggots start crawling under the door.

ELAINE: Oh my god.

RAY: Nasty.

ELAINE: What happened?

JIM: Tried to call but he'd naffed off to Wigan so– Then there's women coming in here complaining, you know, not fair on the other customers. Broke the door in. I've definitely told you this.

ELAINE: Didn't he have a padlock?

JIM: You've got to have some way of getting into the units yourself, could be anything.

RAY: Firearms, drugs, explosives...

JIM: Got a responsibility.

ELAINE: How'd you do it, then?

JIM: Trade secret.

RAY: Won't tell me, either.

JIM: And if I'm not telling dipstick I'm not telling you.

RAY: B sixteen smells a bit like that, though, doesn't it?

ELAINE: Go on, have a look if you can get in…

JIM: What about this dog, then?

RAY: Just– When he came in it was– Funny I remember it but– One of them really really hot days. You know we had that weird heatwave, late September?

JIM: Yes.

RAY: Came in with his dog and I said he couldn't bring it in here–

ELAINE: Why can't you bring a dog in?

JIM: Chew the bubble wrap, gets messy.

RAY: Well I tell him he can't bring it in, and he um he gets a bit shirty, says he can't leave her in the car, she'll get hot and die, hadn't I seen the advert… But he backs down after a second, bloke's sweating like a pig–

ELAINE: How old?

RAY: Bout my age, bit older? Gives in and ties the dog up outside, and you should have heard the racket it made waiting for him…

ELAINE: Probably a young one.

RAY: Made this this horrible whining noise, goes right through you – kind of noise gets you here.

ELAINE: Did you see what he put in?

JIM: Oy, my interrogation, thank you. (*To RAY.*) Did you?

RAY: Not properly. Some kind of big box, I think, had it on a trolley all wrapped in plastic, tape all over it. Didn't see properly cause the dog was there, making the noise so– Thought it might have got run over or something so I went out, and it's just turning round and round on the spot, like it's mental.

ELAINE: So what d'you do? (*To JIM.*) Sorry.

RAY: Well I go in and look for him, and he's doing his padlock up. Yeah, cause I remember he jumped when I. And he looked like he was listening dead hard to what I was saying he was like frowning and nodding loads and sweat on his forehead but we all did that week, and he's just moved this fuckoff big box…

JIM: Yes–

RAY: Yeah so I said I was worried the dog'd do itself an injury, choke itself on the lead or something and then he nods and went a bit white and rushed off.

JIM: OK. And did he look in any way like he might be the kind of bloke runs a kebab van?

RAY: No.

JIM: Or any other kind of perishable foodstuff he might have had in there?

RAY: He was a bit posh actually. Rugby shirt.

JIM: Right.

RAY: But I noticed he had a Cruiser.

ELAINE: What's a Cruiser?

RAY: Big fuckoff padlock. Fort Knox of security accessories.

ELAINE: So he's hiding something.

RAY: I reckon.

ELAINE: Jim, don't you think– I mean if Ray thinks so, he's got the specialist knowledge on padlocks…

JIM: He started padlocks on Monday.

ELAINE: Think you should look.

JIM: Think you should go home.

ELAINE: But what if it's something–

JIM: (*To RAY.*) You wait to mention it now, after–

29

RAY: I know, but– I mean, yeah, he looked a bit shifty but I thought he was just in a piss about the dog, and it– I can't, I mean, it was bastard hot that week, everyone's acting a bit funny, you know?

ELAINE: He's right, it was a bit funny, wasn't it?

JIM: Would you get off home, please?

ELAINE: What if Health and Safety come in, eh, and it turns out you've got a dead dog or something and you chose not to do anything?

RAY: See, I thought about saying something, but then I forgot and I–

ELAINE: They'd close you down.

RAY: Didn't think about it till the smell.

JIM: Right.

RAY: I just remembered it now, so–

ELAINE: D'you have to call the police?

JIM: After I've had a look. RSPCA with any luck.

ELAINE: I think you should. Have a look.

RAY: I'll do it.

JIM: Bollocks will you.

RAY: Thing is–

JIM: What?

RAY: I think I did see a maggot, think I might have stepped on one.

JIM: Bloody hell.

ELAINE: Got a responsibility, haven't you, don't want complaints. Go on, I'll bugger off home if you have a look first. Back in my box.

JIM: Ray, watch the counter.

> *JIM looks out to the carpark.*

You'll go even if it's still raining?

ELAINE: Yep.

JIM: Back in a minute, then.

> *He goes.*

ELAINE: See, that's love for you, anything to get rid of me. You alright?

> *RAY is looking in the direction JIM went off.*

RAY: Yeah, just–

ELAINE: I'd have done the same–

RAY: Yeah, I just–

> *ELAINE leans over the counter and pulls out the box of Celebrations.*

ELAINE: Here, have a chocolate. I won't tell.

> *RAY goes to take one, ELAINE pulls the box away.*

No-no, no choosing – close your eyes and stick your hand in.

> *RAY does so.*

> *Fade.*

SCENE 3

Sunday lunchtime, late September, the hottest day in a freak heatwave. Outside, a car alarm goes off sporadically.

The kitchen of KATE's house. KATE is at the kitchen table, talking on the phone. She wears shorts and a t-shirt, and a baseball cap. There is a laptop computer on the table in front of her.

A dog barks close by.

KATE: Cameron, will you–

> (*Into phone.*) No, it's fine. When you've finished, yeah?
> Cam– Yeah, finish your lunch– No, just– Something to tell
> you, just– No, nothing to worry about – Yeah, yeah, when
> you've finished. Get Dad to wash up. OK. Yeah, Mum, eat
> your lunch. OK. Bye.

KATE hangs up. She wipes sweat off her face and blows on it with her bottom lip sticking out. She looks at the laptop screen, frowning.

The dog barks again.

Shut up, dogshit.

A pause. Then more barking.

Cameron, will you–

Still barking.

Fuck's sake–

KATE leaves the kitchen.

(*Off.*) Will you *shut* (*The dog yelps.*) the *fuck* (*Another yelp.*) up!

Silence. KATE returns, limping slightly. She sits down and clutches her foot in pain, then pulls off a broken toenail.

(*Under her breath.*) Bitch.

She looks at the computer then goes back to it and types furiously.

BEN comes into the kitchen and leans on the work surface. He also wears shorts and a t-shirt. He has a pore-cleansing strip on his nose.

KATE looks at BEN. He points at his nose.

BEN: Chinatown.

KATE: What?

BEN: Chinatown. Jack Nicholson.

KATE: That's a plaster isn't it?

BEN: Have you seen it?

KATE: Before your bollocks dropped, love.

A look.

BEN: What?

KATE: You should ask before you use my bath stuff.

BEN: I didn't think you'd–

KATE: Looks a bit like biting the hand that takes you on holiday / that's all.

BEN: OK.

KATE: Quite expensive those.

BEN: I'll get some more.

KATE: Yeah, with what?

BEN: How much are they?

KATE: I don't know, about a quid each / or something.

BEN: Well, fuck's sake, I'll give you a quid.

KATE: No, it doesn't– I'm just / fucked off.

BEN: Sorry.

BEN sits at the table, opposite KATE.

You OK?

KATE: Busy.

BEN: I mean about yesterday. The girl.

KATE: I'm fine.

BEN: D'you want coffee, tea?

KATE: I'm not traumatised, I'm just fucked off.

BEN: OK. Just thought you might like a coffee, I thought I'd make you one, would you like a coffee?

KATE: You don't ha– OK.

BEN: Cool.

BEN switches the kettle on.

Fucking hot, isn't it?

KATE: Just ask next time, yeah?

BEN: Sorry, yeah.

KATE: Don't have time to go to Boots this week.

BEN: I didn't use the last one, I wouldn't do that.

KATE: God, give him a medal.

BEN: Would you prefer a Coke, actually? Or water, juice?

KATE: Coffee.

BEN: OK.

KATE: *Fucksticks.*

BEN: What?

KATE: Stupid fucking– *Ngh!* All of yesterday lost at the fucking police station, now the cunting thing's crashed on me–

BEN: Switch it off and on again it'll be–

KATE hits the laptop keyboard with her fist.

KATE: Fuck!

BEN: Kate–

KATE: Didn't fucking save it, did I?

BEN: What can I do, can I help you?

KATE: I'm surrounded by fucking–

BEN: Can I help?

KATE: What the fuck help d'you think you could be?

BEN: I don't know, I–

KATE: Keep that fucking animal out of my face, you can do that.

BEN: Sure.

BEN spoons instant coffee into a mug and pours water onto it, then stirs and hands it to KATE.

Why's she in her basket?

KATE: I don't know.

KATE takes a sip of her coffee and makes a face.

BEN: Kate?

KATE: Cause she's tired, cause she's hot? Everyone's hot, it's so hot outside all you can hear is screaming…

BEN: Did you kick her?

KATE: …everything's melting, that car alarm keeps going off and it's not cause anyone's touched it, just the air's so heavy, all the kids shrieking, just think give them a drink of water for fuck's–

BEN: Did you kick her?

KATE: She does that, she goes and hides in her basket, looks all wounded, trying to make you think I / kicked–

35

BEN: Did you kick her?

KATE: No.

BEN: OK. Controlled the impulse.

KATE stands up and puts three more spoonfuls of instant coffee into her mug.

KATE: Stop doing the patient voice, makes you sound like a wanker.

BEN: Thought you were going to try having two spoons, cut down a bit.

KATE: Just as much caffeine in tea.

BEN: I don't have three teabags.

KATE: I didn't sleep it's not– Trying to run a business here. Whole day yesterday shot to shit cause of your stupid mutt. Barking for a walk at nine o'clock on a fucking Saturday.

BEN: I do appreciate it. You walking her, it's–

KATE: Best way to shut her up, isn't it? Glad you managed to sleep through it.

BEN: Sorry.

KATE: *Fucking* thing.

BEN: Can you stop shouting at the / computer–

KATE: What?

BEN: It's alarming, it–

KATE: Won't even let me switch off… *Cunt.*

BEN: Kate.

KATE subsides a little.

Look, I'm sorry about– I'm sorry you ended up walking her, I'm sorry you–

KATE: No, it's fine. Love talking to the police on my day off. Would you leave me / alone?

BEN: Well that's what I came down to say, so–

KATE puts her head in her hands.

Are you OK?

KATE: Just shitloads to do. Massive stack of CVs, candidates with shit-hot qualifications and no social skills that no-one's going to hire, then the forecast for the bank and–

Hate Sundays, make you feel all–

KATE spoons three sugars into her coffee and stirs it. Then she leans across the table and holds the hot spoon from her coffee on BEN's arm.

BEN flinches, but doesn't say anything.

I really hated you last night.

KATE sits back in her chair.

BEN: It was hot. You couldn't sleep either.

KATE: You kept pushing all the blankets over. You were breathing.

BEN: Would you like me to / stop?

KATE: You were breathing *loudly.*

BEN: You were breathing / loudly.

KATE: Only when I was fucked off with you.

BEN puts a hand to his arm.

BEN: That really hurt.

KATE shrugs.

You kept putting the light on…

KATE: See the clock. Have to know the time, how long you're not sleeping for.

BEN: We always used to–

KATE: What?

BEN: When we couldn't sleep. We'd put the light on and chat for a bit.

KATE: Yeah.

BEN: Why don't we do that anymore? We'd sit up and play games, talk about crap, make love even.

KATE: 'Make love'.

BEN: Last night we just lay there getting pissed off with each other.

KATE: When it's hot, isn't it?

BEN: Yeah.

KATE: Makes you irritable.

BEN: Going to be like this all week, they said. Hottest September on record.

BEN peels his shirt off and sniffs it, then pulls a face. Puts it into the washing machine. KATE looks at him. His torso is covered with red marks and bruises.

KATE: You–

BEN: You. Last night.

KATE: That bad?

BEN: You were there.

Get Cameron fed…

BEN takes out a dog bowl and a tin of food. He starts decanting food from the tin with a fork. KATE watches him. After a few moments BEN notices her looking at him.

Babe, it's fine.

BEN comes over and leans down to kiss her. KATE recoils.

What?

KATE: Dog fork. Stinks.

BEN laughs. Puts the fork down on the surface and comes back towards KATE.

I don't want to kiss you it fucking stinks.

BEN goes back to the dog food, continues decanting it, then mashes it with the fork.

D'you have to–

BEN: What?

KATE: You couldn't put your shirt back on, or–

BEN: Too hot.

KATE: OK.

BEN: It's fine in the winter, isn't it, can just cover it all up.

KATE: We could get you summer shirts….

BEN: You could stop.

KATE: I'm–

BEN: I know.

KATE looks at him.

Yeah.

She takes her baseball cap off, runs her hands through her hair.

KATE: Ben, last night…

BEN: Yeah?

KATE: What was it about? I– I can't remember. What it was about.

BEN: The girl under the bush, wasn't it? I think that's what precipitated / it.

39

KATE: Fuck you it wasn't that. Forget it, I've got to get this–

Shit, Ben, I'm so fucking angry. I'm so fucking fucking angry just *fuck* and I don't know–

And after I'm angry I'm just fucking tired, right now I'm…

Beat.

BEN: Hot.

KATE: I don't have time for this, you know?

BEN: Yeah.

KATE: Like, the minute I saw her I was I was like 'shit, how long is this going to fuck things up for?'

BEN: How d'you mean?

KATE: Like– like you know how when something happens and it it comes in the middle of everything and you're trying to, to *feel* to feel the length of it–

BEN: The length of–

KATE: Like how long it's going to disrupt you for…

BEN: OK.

KATE: …and how long you're *expected* to be disrupted for / like–

BEN: I don't–

KATE: Like, grandma's died, so I guess I'll be off work a couple of days, sad for a few weeks, forget about it by two months– But you've got this um, this *dismay* because you know it's got to happen and it buggers up everything, stuff you were trying to get done, and without you having any warning, just everything disrupted and out the window….

BEN: And this was the first thing you thought–

KATE: No, I mean I–

BEN: After you felt sorry for her– You did / feel–

KATE: No, of course I– Of course I felt sorry for her I'm not fucking heartless, I didn't want her, whoever she is, to end up under a bush, *god*, but I didn't I didn't want it to be me and your stupid fucking dog that found her / either.

BEN: It's not Cameron's fault–

KATE: Forget it. / I've got to do this.

BEN: It's not just another reason for you to–

KATE: Ben shut up or I'll get angry. Put a shirt on. Something.

Cameron barks. BEN picks up a rugby shirt from the back of the chair.

BEN: Got that barbecue to go to later.

KATE: Cause the world needs another heat source right now.

KATE sees what BEN is wearing.

You'll be boiling in that.

BEN: You wanted me to put something / on–

KATE: Something that didn't make me feel bad.

BEN: If we go, will you be nice?

KATE: If you wear something / else–

BEN: I'll change before we go, I'm not going upstairs to get something / now–

KATE: Hold me.

Beat.

BEN: It's too hot.

KATE: Please.

He holds her. But it's not a hug, it's boxers holding each other as they pause mid-fight.

BEN: OK?

KATE: Yeah.

Cameron barks again.

Oh, for fuck's–

BEN: Shh. She just wants her food.

BEN puts his hands in the back of KATE's hair and kisses her, hard.

After a moment, KATE pulls away.

KATE: You're all sweaty.

BEN: So are you.

KATE: You stink.

BEN: You want to go upstairs?

KATE: Why?

BEN: We could shower.

KATE: I don't like sex standing up.

BEN: It doesn't have to be sex.

KATE: Last time I gave you a blowjob in the shower I nearly drowned.

BEN: Come on, it's Sunday afternoon, let's go back to bed. We could do the thing I was talking about…

KATE: Ben I've explained, it's just the wrong hole.

They laugh. BEN touches KATE's face. He melts.

BEN: Your eyes…when you laugh…

They're about to kiss again when Cameron barks.

KATE: Shut her up.

BEN: She wants walking.

KATE: She hates me.

BEN: Because you're a bitch to her.

KATE: I walked her yesterday, I tried and she still hates me. She hates that you fuck me and not her.

BEN: Kate, you can't act like a world-class cunt and then expect people / to–

KATE: Dogs–

BEN: People *or* dogs. You can't behave like that poor dead girl existed only to

The phone rings.

fuck up your weekend–

KATE picks up the phone. She holds eye contact with BEN as she speaks into it.

KATE: Hi Mum. Cause your number comes up on the– Caller Display, yeah. You finished lunch? Yeah, I – Yeah, pretty good. Found a dead body in the park yesterday then I've been getting some work done today and we're going to a barbecue ton– Yeah. Some girl under a bush. I don't know, eighteen, nineteen. Yeah. Walking Cameron. I do walk her some– No, not a prostitute, looked like a waitress or something, black skirt, white shirt, sensible shoes, you know? Didn't identify her yet, this was only yesterday, so– Police kept me for hours, statements and– It was on the news. I was 'a woman walking her dog in Newbold Park'. Wanted to call the channel and say 'It's not my fucking dog, it's his fucking dog, I only walked it cause I can't sleep through the Saturday morning barking festival...

How's Dad?

BEN picks up Cameron's dog food bowl and goes out.

Had her throat slit. I know. Really straight cut across. Something really fucking sharp. Hardly any blood, though, like it all went into the ground or her hair, hardly any on her shirt…

It was surreal.

I think surreal. Never know if I'm using that word right…

It's weird, it's details, things you keep seeing. Like I noticed I had dirt up my fingernails, just a second before, and I hoped the dog wasn't going to the bush to have a shit because then I'd have to pick it up in the bag and carry it to the next– And when I saw her I thought, well first I thought fuck you, dogshit, thanks for that, that's my day fucked, isn't it?

No, I did feel sorry for her. I just– there's loads to do with the company, and– I'm not overdoing it, this is– You have to work at the weekend when you run your own business. And now they want me back in tomorrow for more statements so that's half a day's work lost…

BEN comes back with blood on his hand. He looks at KATE.

So it was weird, anyway. Yeah.

BEN: Hang up.

Beat.

KATE: Mum– Mum, can I call you later in the week? Yeah, Ben needs me, I– OK. Love you too.

KATE hangs up and looks at BEN.

BEN: How hard d'you have to fucking kick her to draw blood?

KATE: I didn't–

BEN: Show me your shoes.

KATE: What?

BEN: Show me your shoes / the ones on your feet–

KATE: No, I'm not–

BEN lunges at KATE, a kind of rugby tackle in which she falls to the ground and BEN rips the flip-flops from her feet. He examines her toes, and the shoes.

BEN: So what's this red stuff, then, ketchup?

KATE: You didn't see me / do–

BEN: She's hiding in her basket, scared shitless and she's got a cut on her side, you've got blood under your toenails, it's not rocket, is it?

KATE doesn't say anything. Looks at the floor.

BEN pauses a moment then looks as if he will lash out at KATE with her shoe. Instead, he turns and aims a savage blow at the kitchen work surface.

KATE: What you doing?

BEN: Moral fucking high ground.

Another blow to the work surface.

I'm going to give her this as a fucking chew toy.

KATE gets up.

I think you should apologise.

Pause.

KATE: I'm sorry.

BEN: To Cameron.

KATE: She doesn't unders–

BEN: I want you on your knees in front of her.

KATE: Fine, OK.

BEN: On your knees.

KATE: Yeah.

BEN: Now, before I walk her, if she's up to–

KATE: Fuck's sake.

KATE moves to leave.

Do I have to bark or will English do?

BEN: She'll understand.

KATE goes out. BEN opens a drawer, takes out the dog lead. A moment.

You on your knees in there?

KATE comes back in. Goes towards the laptop.

KATE: This is fucking–

BEN: What?

KATE: Fucking ridiculous I'm not apologising to the bloody *dog*–

KATE laughs.

Idiot.

She looks at him, sees he's glaring at her.

Look, I'm sorry, OK, I got– Babe, come here…

She motions for him to come closer to her, to lean down to kiss her. As he's leaning in she rips the pore strip off his nose, laughing.

BEN: Ow–

KATE: You can't stand there and say things with that on, you look like a twat.

She examines the strip.

Oh my god, look at this, fucking disgusting like you ooze this kind of–

BEN grabs KATE by her hair, twists his hand into the back of it and pulls her up until she's standing.

Ow, fuck, Ben–

BEN: Why d'you have to be so fucking–

KATE: I–

BEN: How did I end up with such a fucking–

KATE: Ben–

BEN: What, does it, does this hurt?

KATE: Yes.

BEN: Does it hurt like your fucking fingernails, like boiling water, like the way you look at me / when you're–

KATE: I don't / know.

BEN: No, you don't know, you don't fucking know.

KATE: OK, I–

BEN: You've got to fucking stop, Kate. D'you have any idea what this fucking *does*? I never fucking heal my bruises have got bruises on them I'm always–

KATE: Leave if you–

BEN: What?

KATE: You can–

BEN: What?

KATE: Leave if you–

BEN: I can't fucking–

KATE: Fucking *leave*–

> *KATE grabs her coffee cup from the table and hurls it at the wall.*

BEN: I can't I can't you know I fucking can't I haven't got *anything* I'm fucking staying but–

KATE: Let me go–

BEN: But you're making it *really* / difficult to–

KATE: Fuck you–

BEN: If you push me, if you really push me, you know I'm stronger. I could snap you in two if I wanted to and I don't want to I really don't want to but this is no way to *live,* Kate…

KATE flails, tries to kick him.

…and you try and say it's the girl, it's because of the girl, it's not the girl you're always like this and it's got to fucking *stop.*

He shakes her hard.

KATE: Stop!

He stops shaking her, but keeps hold.

BEN: Are we going to stop or carry on?

KATE: Stop.

BEN: We're choosing now, we're going to stop this, yeah?

KATE: Yeah.

BEN: We're going to be like normal people, go out for dinner and shit, yeah?

KATE: Yeah.

BEN: See our friends like normal fucking people.

KATE: Yeah.

BEN: OK.

BEN releases KATE's hair. KATE looks at the floor.

Look at me.

KATE looks up at him.

You're a fucking bitch but I / love you.

KATE: You've got hair in your hand.

BEN looks down at his hand – there's a clump of hair in it.

KATE puts her hand to the back of her head.

You pulled a whole clump out.

BEN: That's what it feels like.

KATE: Fuck that hurt.

BEN: This is for you to learn.

Go and apologise to Cameron.

KATE: What– I backed / down for–

BEN: Learn, Kate.

KATE moves away.

KATE: OK.

She frowns.

Fuckit Ben–

Her fists clench and she goes back to BEN and punches him squarely in the back. He reels.

BEN: Fucking –

KATE: God all-fucking mighty you're so full of shit. I'm not apologising to your fucking dog.

BEN: You said we were going to–

KATE: Fuck you.

KATE goes out. BEN picks up the dog lead, whips it fiercely at the table, then looks at it in his hand. Looks after KATE.

BEN: Fine.

He follows her out, twisting the dog lead in his hand.

Fade.

SCENE 4

Tuesday evening, mid-January, dark already, getting cold.

The garage at JIM's house. JIM sits cross-legged on the floor, carefully removing the screws from a brass door handle. Beside him, underneath a camping groundsheet, is a pile of doors.

ELAINE calls from inside the house.

ELAINE: I'm home, love.

> *She enters the doorway to the garage. She is wearing Green Door Self-Storage dungarees underneath her outdoor coat.*
>
> *JIM doesn't look up, but continues with the handle.*

Born in a barn?

JIM: What?

ELAINE: Doesn't– How you feeling, good day?

JIM: Alright.

ELAINE: OK well alright's better than yesterday–

JIM: Not great.

ELAINE: OK. But– Working towards great, that's the thing, isn't it?

JIM: Uh-huh.

ELAINE: Trying.

JIM: Yep.

> *JIM stops. Puts the handle down. Looks up at ELAINE. She's taking her coat off.*

Look at you.

ELAINE: Thought I'd– you know, try and look like the rest. Not the boss-lady or anything, cause I keep having to ask how to do things so that wouldn't work…

What d'you think?

JIM: Yeah. Suits you.

ELAINE: Great.

JIM frowns.

No, you're right, that's usually the right answer. Just– (*Exhales.*) Need a bath, my feet hate me for being in flat shoes all day…

I picked up the prescription…

ELAINE fumbles in her bag and pulls out a pharmacy packet.

JIM: Ta.

JIM takes the bottle and looks at the label. He turns the lid of the bottle and the safety catch clicks.

ELAINE: Here–

ELAINE takes the bottle and unscrews it successfully. She hands it back to JIM.

JIM: Not going to sleep yet, am I?

ELAINE: Screw it back on then. What you doing?

JIM: Fixing things.

ELAINE: Jim the front door was wide open, didn't you–

ELAINE smiles.

D'you remember, with Danny?

'Yes, dad, I *was* born in a barn, cause I'm Jesus'. Remember?

Should keep it closed though, really. Security.

Did the boys ring?

JIM: No.

ELAINE: No. Well, only two weeks since they were here, wasn't it? Spect they will soon. Check up on you.

JIM doesn't reply.

I brought Ray back. Can he come in and see you?

JIM: You've got him waiting outside?

ELAINE: No– he's–

JIM: Queuing.

ELAINE: He's in the kitchen. I wanted to check with you first.

JIM: Out in the waiting room...

ELAINE: Thought you might like a bit of– you know, not just me. Can I get him?

JIM shrugs.

OK.

ELAINE goes back into the house through the doorway. A moment later she comes back to the doorframe and stands in it, frowning. She runs a hand over where the hinges used to be attached.

You've taken the door off.

JIM: Yep.

ELAINE: Are you, what, fixing it?

JIM: Open plan. Nicer without the door.

ELAINE: OK.

Beat.

What if, what about when I'm in there cooking and I want my music on, you're in here wanting peace and quiet?

OK.

ELAINE goes back into the house. JIM scratches his head, then rubs the palms of his hands on his forehead. He puts a finger to one nostril and blows really hard, then does the same on the other side. He then blows hard down both nostrils, concentrating.

ELAINE comes back into the doorway.

You've taken all the doors off.

JIM: Yep.

ELAINE: What've you–

JIM pulls the groundsheet off the pile of doors. There are nine.

How long did that take you?

JIM: Bout ten minutes each.

ELAINE: But wh– OK.

Ray?

RAY appears in the doorway.

RAY: Alright Boss?

JIM nods. RAY steps into the garage.

ELAINE: He's taken all the doors off.

RAY: Yeah, what d'you use?

JIM: Electric screwdriver.

RAY: Yeah, Black & Decker?

JIM: Bosch.

RAY: I'm getting a DeWalt next week. Upgrading.

ELAINE: Ten minutes per door. Take me hours.

RAY: Nah, when you've got the right tools it–

JIM looks at RAY. An uncomfortable pause.

ELAINE: We heard this thing on the radio this morning, this story, what was it, Ray?

RAY: Um–

ELAINE: The one about the man–

RAY: Yeah, there's this man–

ELAINE: With the lifts–

RAY: Oh, yeah, this– this bloke ran a company made lifts–

ELAINE: For office buildings and things.

RAY: Yeah and he was forty and he suddenly got, um, claustrophobia.

ELAINE: And vertigo.

RAY: So he couldn't, you know, he couldn't go inside his lifts anymore. And the company was going to go bust if he didn't sort it out so he got um, he got–

ELAINE: Therapy.

RAY: Yeah. And he got better.

ELAINE: And now they even make glass lifts. And we thought–

RAY: Boss, we've eaten all your chocolates. She found your stash.

ELAINE: Ray–

RAY: Sorry.

ELAINE: I'm going to– I'll be inside, OK?

RAY: Was that alright?

ELAINE: Yes.

ELAINE goes out. RAY stands awkwardly looking at JIM. JIM holds the pill bottle and clicks the cap round and round.

JIM: It true that story?

RAY: Yeh. I mean I– I didn't hear it myself, in and out the office like a bull in a cuckoo clock… What's that?

JIM: Nothing.

JIM puts the pill bottle to one side.

Going all right, customers in?

RAY: Yeah, good few. For– Y'know, for January.

JIM: She doing alright?

RAY: Yeah.

She's not a not a natural sales person, really. Trying to get her to shift more padlocks.

JIM: Right.

RAY: Keep having to show her how to do the accounts, she can't remember.

JIM: Right.

RAY: She knows, she says she's not the right man for the job really… I mean, she doesn't mind filling in and–

JIM: Yeah.

RAY: Least it's January so it's quiet.

Pause.

You, um, you coming back then?

JIM: Don't know.

RAY: Elaine's been telling them you've got glandular fever.

RAY points at JIM's pile of door handles.

Help you with that?

JIM: If you want.

RAY sits down on the pile of doors and picks up a handle and a screwdriver.

RAY: Quite good really, cause glandular fever takes ages so–

JIM: Can do.

RAY: She wants me to ask you to come in tomorrow, quick visit.

JIM: No.

RAY: I told her it's all under control, I can handle it till you get back, and if she's there, for official decision making, bit like the queen, you know…

JIM: She's in charge.

RAY: Course, yeah.

She just said I should ask, cause of it being four weeks– Says it's long enough, you know? Pass us another–

JIM passes RAY another door handle. RAY gestures towards the doors.

Why'd you um–

JIM: Oh, you know–

RAY: Meant to tell you – I worked it out.

JIM: What?

RAY: How to get into the units without the key. Trade secret. Worked it out myself.

JIM: Right.

RAY: S'alright I won't / tell her–

JIM: Don't need me at all then.

RAY: No, I – I mean it took ages it–

JIM: Keep thinking about her…

RAY: Elaine?

JIM: The woman. In the box.

RAY: Oh.

JIM: See her all the time. Red marks round her– (*Puts his hand to his neck.*). Stuffed in that box, all twisted up, big red mark round her neck, she looked, what was left of her, she looked pissed off. Her own dog lead I mean– You know? I– All that hair. She fucking stank and– the maggots and–

I keep thinking–

Beat. JIM looks at the floor.

RAY: She, um, she keeps crying. Elaine, she–

Pass us another.

JIM: All done now.

A long pause. ELAINE appears at the door to the garage.

There's these little fish, right…

RAY: Um–

JIM: I keep wondering if – Like maybe if I hadn't found her, maybe she wouldn't have been dead.

RAY: I don't really–

ELAINE and RAY exchange a look.

JIM: There's these little fish, little black ones and if you want to look at them you have to let them swim into your eye, like you have to put your head in the tank, in the water and–

JIM sees ELAINE out of the corner of his eye.

Hello, love.

So I put my head in the tank and let these fish swim into my eye and I could see them but then once I'd once I'd finished looking and took my head out it– It turned out one of the fish had swum behind my eye and got stuck and there's this optician trying to get it out with some kind of metal probe thing but when it finally flopped out this little black fish was bleeding and– Dead.

RAY: When was this?

ELAINE: It didn't happen.

RAY: Didn't know fish had blood.

ELAINE: It's a dream or…

JIM: Maybe in that second when I opened the box, maybe–
Like if I hadn't, maybe she'd have turned up at home a
few days later, she'd have– Maybe she– I don't know, just
wanted to disappear for a bit.

Maybe she'd have turned up at home, couple of days
later, she'd have just said 'I'm sorry. I needed some time
so I– I went to the seaside to think. And I'm sorry I didn't
call and I know you must have been really worried. But I
looked out at the sea and I knew I loved you so I've come
back. And I'm sorry it took a trip to Cleethorpes to get me
straightened out.'

RAY: Bit complicated / isn't it?

JIM: She went away to Cleethorpes to have a think, and if I
hadn't been there to find her in that box, she'd have come
back but the minute I saw her, that was it.

ELAINE: (*To RAY.*) Is he coming in?

JIM: No.

RAY: He says no.

ELAINE: We could say you didn't want to overdo it, maybe
the doctor said you had to be careful, take it slowly.

JIM: No.

RAY: Not sure if he's–

ELAINE: Cause you have to take it slowly with glandular
fever, so that's alright. Next week, maybe, just for a little
bit?

JIM: No.

ELAINE: Have a think about it at least.

JIM: I'm not going in.

Pause.

ELAINE: Did / you–

RAY: I should–

ELAINE: OK.

RAY goes to leave. ELAINE catches his hand as he goes.

Thanks, Ray.

ELAINE watches RAY go. Then she comes further into the garage and sits by JIM.

Come on a bit, hasn't he?

She tries to touch JIM's hair, but he jerks away.

Did you eat anything? I left your lunch in the fridge.

JIM: Not hungry.

ELAINE: OK. Well, you're– you're used to being so active, aren't you, probably burning less fuel… Pity, cause the freezer's stuffed with food we never ate at Christmas, what with the boys only being here a couple of days / instead of…

JIM: I can't stand the smell.

ELAINE: Just a turkey sandwich.

JIM: I've got the smell up my nose.

ELAINE: What smell?

JIM: B sixteen.

ELAINE sighs.

ELAINE: Right.

JIM: Just outside the door, and inside opening the box, my lungs got full of– Sticks like tar, it's stuck to the inside of

59

my nose I can't get– Like one of the maggots crawled up and got stuck.

Beat.

ELAINE: Have you tried Vicks?

JIM: What?

ELAINE: I don't know, it might–

JIM: Not that kind of–

ELAINE: Just cause it's a strong smell, you know, it might– Or that Olbas Oil, same kind of thing, really.

JIM: Have you never– Got something stuck, a smell?

ELAINE: Not that I remember.

I mean, physically, it's not– I mean, is it?

JIM: I don't know *physically*.

ELAINE: Well it might help if you actually do something.

Beat.

But this is good.

JIM: What?

ELAINE: Talking about it. That's the thing, isn't it, talking about it?

JIM: Is it?

ELAINE: Well, that's the way it'll get better, isn't it?

JIM: I don't feel better.

ELAINE: You might have to talk about it more.

JIM shakes his head.

Might take some time.

JIM: I don't want to–

ELAINE: Jim.

JIM: I don't want to talk to Ray about it.

ELAINE: Just it was not talking about it buggered Christmas up, wasn't it?

Beat.

I'm here.

JIM looks away. ELAINE takes his hand. He pulls it away. ELAINE takes it again. They wrestle with their hands until ELAINE is only holding JIM's little finger. He lets her hang on, but turns the rest of himself away from her. He looks around the garage.

JIM: Never sat on the floor in here before. That thing where you see something from an angle you've never seen it before it all looks weird and...

ELAINE closes her eyes.

When I went in there– I felt– There was that smell and– It. It smelled a bit like. Sex. Like a room where you've been having sex. And I–

JIM looks at ELAINE.

You've got your eyes shut.

ELAINE opens her eyes.

ELAINE: No, just–

JIM: Why've you got your eyes shut?

ELAINE: I– Just listening.

JIM: I'm not saying any more.

ELAINE: I'm sorry. Please. Eyes open.

JIM: You think it's–

ELAINE: I just shut my eyes for a second, I'm sorry, I was listening. Please, I'll keep them open...

JIM: Right.

ELAINE: It smelled like–

JIM: Sex, yes.

ELAINE: I was letting you say it.

JIM: You didn't want to / say it.

ELAINE: I was letting you. It smelled like sex.

JIM: Yeah. And I got–

ELAINE: Did you?

JIM: Yeah.

JIM takes his hand away from ELAINE.

Sorry.

ELAINE: No– I don't–

JIM: And when I opened the box I was still– And I saw her– And I felt–

Pause.

I felt– I felt like– Elaine, I felt like I was the centre of the universe. I couldn't– I couldn't believe how how *important* I was. Less than a minute, standing there looking at her, hair all over her pissed-off face and I felt I felt I felt like a god.

ELAINE: God.

Silence.

JIM: I touched something, or– Or I was touched, I don't / know–

ELAINE: You touched her?

JIM: No I didn't bloody touch her, course I didn't–

Not saying any more.

Silence. JIM picks up the pill bottle and clicks the cap round and round.

ELAINE: Alright then. Can I say something?

I'm a bit– I'm a little bit sick of this. You let this mess up all of Christmas, our only time with the boys till what, a couple of days at Easter if we're lucky and you hardly said a word to anyone you'd barely look at them and I don't know if you noticed from in there but it was awful, Jim.

Cause bless them, they tried – taking you out to the pub and– and you just stared into your pint for an hour, no wonder they both went off straight after Boxing Day…

Will you stop clicking that, please?

JIM stops. He puts the bottle of pills on top of the pile of doors.

I mean I feel like. I feel like you're letting this get in the way when it really– It's a bit. I'm a bit– the doors and the talking rubbish about fish in your eyes and– I'm sorry it happened but I won't take responsibility and you shouldn't because we had nothing to do with it and we're not people that kill people and we're not–

I don't think you're trying. I can't believe how *unimportant* I–

Jim?

JIM: All feels a bit–

ELAINE: Bit what?

No answer.

A bit what?

JIM shakes his head. Beat.

I don't care about the business, if you don't want it anymore, fine, we'll sell it I don't care. But you'll have to do something else. You can't just stay at home taking the place apart with a screwdriver.

Jim, you've got to put the doors back. I won't be lonely, I can't do it.

JIM nods.

Will you?

JIM: What?

ELAINE: Put the doors back.

JIM: Bit tired from taking them all off, to be honest.

ELAINE: Right.

JIM: And I might sleep. If they're not there, if they're safe in here.

ELAINE: Oh god.

JIM: Cause I can't sleep, you see / and that's–

ELAINE: I know. But you've got your pills now so–

ELAINE puts her hands to her face.

JIM: Sorry.

ELAINE: Not sorry Jim, just do something.

ELAINE goes towards the door.

JIM: Put them back tomorrow.

ELAINE goes out. JIM remains on the floor and blows down each nostril in turn, as before. As he's doing so he catches sight of the bottle of pills on top of the doors.

Fade.

SCENE 5

Friday morning, late September, sunny with a heatwave starting tomorrow.

A hotel room, the same as in Scene 1.

Someone is lying in the bed, the sheets pulled up high. The figure is motionless.

AMY comes into the room with clean towels over her arm and a plastic carry-case of cleaning fluids.

She stops short when she sees the figure in the bed.

AMY: Oh god, sorry.

> *She goes to back out of the room, then stops again. She turns back slowly for a longer look at the figure in the bed.*

> Right.

> God not again.

> *She looks away. Bites her lip.*

> You're supposed to put the Do Not Disturb on. Then I wouldn't come barging in.

> *AMY takes a breath and goes over to the bed. She lifts the sheet and looks under it.*

> *Suddenly the figure moves, sits up, shouts, jumps out of bed. This is CHARLIE. He's just wearing boxer shorts.*

> *AMY gasps, backs away.*

CHARLIE: Who the fuck are / you?

AMY: Shit *fuck* sorry–

> *AMY backs away to the door.*

> Shit.

She leans against the door, her hand to her mouth, looking at CHARLIE. He's disarmingly attractive.

Sorry.

CHARLIE: What the fuck are you–

AMY: Sorry, house– housekeeping. You didn't put the– You didn't put the Do Not Disturb sign on I– And–

CHARLIE: What, you normally come and lift the sheets off people, did– Did you not see me? (*Looks at his watch.*) Shit–

AMY: What?

CHARLIE: Missed my alarm.

CHARLIE picks up his alarm clock.

Didn't set my alarm.

He looks at AMY. Sees she's still flattened against the door. Puts the clock down and takes a step towards her.

God, are you–

AMY: I thought you were dead.

CHARLIE: God, I– I mean crikey that'd be awful, wouldn't it?

AMY: You had the sheet pulled up over you, I–

CHARLIE: I I I always do, I–

AMY: I mean it looked–

CHARLIE: Why would you think I was dead?

AMY: Because–

CHARLIE: I mean, it must happen, but–

AMY: It happens quite a lot.

Beat.

Sorry. Come back later.

CHARLIE: It happens to you?

AMY: Sorry?

CHARLIE: It happens to you quite a lot?

AMY: Yes.

CHARLIE: Shit.

AMY: What?

CHARLIE: It, um, sorry, it suddenly occurs to me I'm just standing here in my boxers.

AMY looks away.

AMY: Sorry. I'll–

AMY puts her hand on the doorknob, to leave.

CHARLIE: No, hang on, wait. Don't–

AMY: Do the other rooms and come back I–

CHARLIE: No, just let me– I– I want to, you know, sort this out, I just think it'd be better if I had trousers on, if you could just–

CHARLIE goes to the wardrobe and opens it, takes out a pair of trousers.

If you could just hang on a second–

AMY: You can say at Reception–

CHARLIE: Sorry?

CHARLIE pulls the trousers on.

AMY: The manager's behind Reception this morning if you want to / complain.

CHARLIE: I don't. I don't want to complain.

AMY: Really?

CHARLIE: No. Yes, really.

I'm sorry I jumped out of bed shouting, I mean I was I was alarming, you were just as alarmed as I was / if not more...

AMY: Oh no, it's–

CHARLIE: I mean, if I'd managed to set my alarm for the right time – If I hadn't got totally sketched last night, completely knocked myself out–

AMY: Yeah.

CHARLIE: Just missing my alarm – that's what I'm pissed off about, not about you, you're–

CHARLIE looks at AMY.

God.

AMY: What?

CHARLIE: Nothing.

He holds his hand out to shake hers.

Charlie.

AMY: Amy.

Hi.

She shakes his hand.

CHARLIE: Pleasure to meet you.

AMY: Ooh–

CHARLIE: What?

AMY: Warm hands.

They smile at each other. She lets go of his hand.

Sorry.

I'll come back later.

CHARLIE: No, you can do it–

AMY: You'll not get any breakfast now, they stop at ten.

CHARLIE: Do you mind if I–

AMY: What?

CHARLIE: If I stick around while you–

AMY: Oh. Um, OK. It's not very interesting to watch, I–
OK.

You're here another night, yeah?

CHARLIE: Yeah.

AMY: OK.

CHARLIE: That makes a difference to–

AMY: If you're leaving I change the sheets.

CHARLIE: Course.

AMY smiles at him.

She takes a duster and polish from her cleaning kit and wipes the surfaces in the room. CHARLIE takes a shirt from the wardrobe and puts it on. He watches her out of the corner of his eye.

A slightly uncomfortable pause. AMY fills it.

AMY: Where'd you go?

CHARLIE: Sorry?

AMY: Last night, where'd you go, was it somewhere in town?

CHARLIE: Um, god it was– (*Thinking.*) Sorry, hungover, um– Cocktail place, hammered metal lizards on the walls–

AMY: Iguana Bar.

CHARLIE: Yeah. Pretty shit, actually.

AMY: Don't go at the weekend, get your bum pinched five times on the way to the loo.

CHARLIE: Well, I don't usually–

AMY: Town's a shithole, I'm afraid.

CHARLIE: Kind of place Dante'd draw circles round.

AMY: Who?

CHARLIE: Circles of hell, you know, the– the picture?

He draws circles in the air with his finger.

Beat.

So you find dead people quite often.

AMY: Not like Beachy Head or anything, not like it happens every day, or– Not like it happens to anyone else, either, just– My mum said I should maybe move to Beachy Head, get a job at that hotel there, says they'd be used to people like me–

CHARLIE: How many times?

AMY: Well. Two.

CHARLIE: Fuck.

AMY: So not that many really, just–

CHARLIE: No but *two*. That's got to be– I mean, god is that *usual* for a hotel?

AMY: I don't think there's official figures–

CHARLIE: No, course. But– God, but I mean it's fascinating to think, isn't it, all those hotels all over the country, all over the world, all those people booking in to die, it's–

AMY: I don't like to–

CHARLIE: No. Sure, no. Kind of sick.

AMY: Well it's only two.

CHARLIE: Before and after, though, isn't it? The way you–

CHARLIE breaks off, looks at AMY.

God–

AMY: What?

CHARLIE: Nothing, you're– Sorry, you're– Um, beautiful.

AMY: Oh, I'm–

CHARLIE: No, you are.

AMY: I'm in my stupid tabard, I–

CHARLIE: I'm sorry, I don't normally say things to– Sorry, do you / mind?

AMY: No, I– No.

Sorry, not supposed to argue when people say things… My mum says you should always just say thank you when someone says something.

Sorry I keep talking about my mum, do it when I'm nervous.

CHARLIE: Just thought I should say, so– Well, didn't think, really. Just said.

They smile at each other. He tries to hold her gaze but she looks away, moves to tidy around the tea tray.

AMY: You're not a tea drinker, then?

CHARLIE: Sorry?

AMY: You didn't touch the–

CHARLIE: Oh, no. Coffee, really.

AMY: Some coffee there.

CHARLIE: Can't drink instant.

AMY: Right.

CHARLIE: Most places I stay you can just call down for an espresso so–

AMY: Wow. Room service.

CHARLIE: Yeah.

AMY: Like five stars?

CHARLIE: Yeah.

AMY: Wow. I'd love to be in a five star hotel.

CHARLIE: Don't know if the pay's any better–

AMY: Stay in one.

CHARLIE: Right. You should.

AMY: Can't afford it.

CHARLIE: Someone should take you.

I'll take you.

AMY: You're joking.

CHARLIE: Up to you.

AMY: No, you're joking.

CHARLIE: I don't do jokes.

Again, AMY breaks his gaze, goes back to dusting.

AMY: Shame. Girls like a sense of humour.

CHARLIE: Thing is the um, the only kind of jokes I can ever remember are a bit, um a bit sick.

AMY: Like what?

CHARLIE: Um, no it's a bit sick.

AMY: Go on.

CHARLIE: No, I–

AMY: OK, I'll finish up later, then, leave you in / peace.

She goes to leave.

CHARLIE: What d'you get if you put a baby in a blender?

AMY: What?

CHARLIE: What d'you get if you put a baby in a blender?

AMY: What?

CHARLIE: A stiffy.

Beat.

AMY: That is a bit sick.

CHARLIE: Yeah. Sorry.

AMY stifles a giggle.

AMY: Just do the bathroom.

AMY takes the towels, plus a bottle of cleaning spray and a cloth into the bathroom. CHARLIE sits on the bed.

He stands and goes towards his suitcase and stretches his hand out towards it, then stops.

Looks towards the bathroom. Moves away from the suitcase, his hand on the back of his neck.

A moment, then he goes back to the suitcase rapidly and takes out a shallow, rectangular black box. He puts it down on the bedside table, touches the top of the box then moves away again.

Looks towards the bathroom.

CHARLIE: What was it like, finding those people?

AMY comes to the bathroom door.

AMY: Pardon?

CHARLIE: Was it terrible, when you found those people, the dead ones?

AMY: Oh right.

AMY goes back into the bathroom.

It was– It kind of wasn't, it was kind of normal. D'you think that's awful?

CHARLIE: No.

AMY comes back to the bathroom door.

AMY: Pardon?

CHARLIE: I said no. It's not awful. If that's how you felt.

AMY: I felt old, mostly.

AMY goes back into the bathroom and carries on cleaning.

Just get on with it, don't you?

CHARLIE sits down on the edge of the bed with the box on his lap. He opens it and takes out a Japanese carving knife with an ornate horn and ebony handle. He handles it with some confidence, but you can tell it's incredibly sharp.

I mean, yeah, the first one was really hard, I'd never seen a dead person before and she was really– really young. Like my age.

CHARLIE: Christ.

CHARLIE looks towards the bathroom door, the knife in his hand.

AMY: Right mess, as well. Sick all over the sheets and blood and stuff…

Actually the second one was worse, he was older, he was a dad and it wasn't that long after the first one so I hadn't really got over that yet and now it's like, like a pattern...

CHARLIE puts the knife back in the box, puts it quietly back on the dressing table.

Manager thinks I'm the angel of death or something, won't let me work on Bank Holidays now. Quite a relief when you sat up and swore at me, really.

AMY comes out of the bathroom.

All done.

She sees the black box on the dressing table.

What's that?

CHARLIE stands up.

CHARLIE: It's– I uh– It's a product I'm delivering to a client today.

AMY: A product?

CHARLIE: I um, I supply kitchen equipment.

AMY: Pots and pans.

CHARLIE: Special, hand made stuff.

AMY: Can I see?

CHARLIE: I um. Yeah.

CHARLIE holds the box open towards AMY.

AMY: It's a knife.

CHARLIE: Yeah.

AMY: A kitchen knife?

CHARLIE: Yes.

AMY: Doesn't look like a kitchen knife.

CHARLIE: It's for a special kind of Japanese cuisine. More about worship than practicality, really.

AMY: Can I hold it?

CHARLIE: It's fucking sharp.

AMY: OK.

AMY takes out the knife and holds it. CHARLIE has to sit down.

CHARLIE: Beautiful, yeah?

AMY: Pattern on it. Looks like wood, not metal.

CHARLIE: Multi-layered steel. Hand-forged. Breath–
Breathtakingly sharp.

CHARLIE looks up, sees AMY looking at him intently.

What?

AMY: You're all lit up, your eyes are shining.

CHARLIE: Oh. Right, I–

AMY: It's nice.

They smile at each other. AMY puts the knife back in the box.

Do the bed now–

CHARLIE: Right.

AMY: Last thing.

CHARLIE moves awkwardly from the bed to the stool by the dressing table. AMY goes to the bed and starts to make it.

CHARLIE takes his shoes and socks and starts to put them on, watching AMY.

There isn't really anything to say. He keeps watching her after he's done his shoes and socks. She knows he's watching and occasionally smiles – it's nice to have someone there.

CHARLIE: OK.

AMY: What?

CHARLIE: Should get some breakfast.

AMY: You're going?

CHARLIE: Get something to eat. Suddenly hungry.

AMY: I could get chef to do you a bacon sarnie. Egg on toast.

CHARLIE picks up his wallet and keys.

CHARLIE: Might pop into town.

AMY: OK. Good luck.

CHARLIE goes to leave.

CHARLIE: Meet me later.

AMY: I–

CHARLIE: Get a drink or something.

AMY: I can't, I've got to wait on in the restaurant, then I'm on bar all evening, we're a bit short-staffed–

CHARLIE: What time d'you finish?

AMY: Midnight.

CHARLIE: A drink at midnight, then. Celebration drink.

AMY: I don't–

CHARLIE: Maybe we've broken the pattern, you know – maybe you'll never find another one–

AMY: Oh don't–

CHARLIE: What?

AMY: Tempting fate.

CHARLIE: Bugger fate, you know? I'd take you somewhere nice.

AMY: No, I– I'll be tired, I should go home. But thanks.

CHARLIE: Tomorrow, then?

AMY: On till midnight again.

CHARLIE: What time d'you start?

AMY: Breakfast. Eight o'clock.

CHARLIE: Long day.

AMY: I'm sorry, just– You're a guest. Not allowed. Already sailing close to the–

CHARLIE: What about early – tomorrow morning, early? No-one around then.

AMY: I can't–

CHARLIE: Coffee or a walk in the park or something? Or– Or I don't know. Just I've got to head off tomorrow.

You know, I wake up this morning and it turns out I'm not dead, and that's– I mean, isn't it? That's remarkable, surely. And if I wake up tomorrow not dead I'd like to see you before I leave. Cause who knows – you know, tomorrow I might crash the Boxster, wrap it round a lamp post. Or a pedestrian. And I like you a lot.

AMY: A Boxster.

CHARLIE: Porsche.

AMY: I know.

CHARLIE: You'd look great in it. See it if you look out.

AMY goes to the curtains and looks at the car park.

The silver one. Convertible.

What d'you think? Meet me at seven tomorrow, a drive if you like, or a walk in the park, don't have to decide now… It's going to be a gorgeous day – hottest September on record, they're saying. You should get out in it.

AMY: OK.

CHARLIE: Yes?

AMY: Yeah.

CHARLIE comes close to AMY, looks into her eyes.

CHARLIE: You're luminous.

AMY frowns.

You glow.

CHARLIE kisses his thumb and places it on AMY's forehead.

Tomorrow.

AMY nods. CHARLIE leaves.

AMY finishes making the bed. She catches sight of the knife box on the bedside table, and looks to the door to check CHARLIE isn't coming back. Then, she opens the box and looks at the knife. She touches it with her fingertips, but doesn't take it out of the box.

AMY closes the box and looks around her. She starts to dust again, smiling, distracted, looking at the door CHARLIE went through, not noticing she's cleaned the surfaces already. After a few seconds she gives in and decides to enjoy the moment.

She sits down on the edge of the bed and laughs to herself, quietly, her hand to her mouth.

The end.